Those People in Washington

By David Flitner

Illustrated by William Neebe

 CHILDRENS PRESS, CHICAGO

To my sister, Jinny

Library of Congress Cataloging in Publication Data

Flitner, David.
   Those people in Washington.

    SUMMARY: An easy-to-read introduction to the
history, organization, and operations of the federal
government.
    1. United States—Politics and government—
Juvenile literature. [1. United States—Politics
and government] I. Neebe, William, illus.
II. Title.
JK34.F54   320.4'73   72-13220
ISBN 0-516-03626-2

1 2 3 4 5 6 7 8 9 10 11 12 13 14 15 16 17 18 19 20 21 22 23 24 25 R 75 74 73

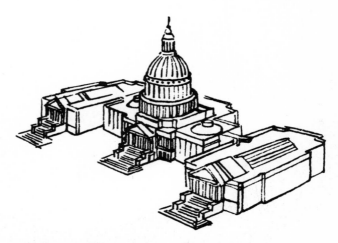

THOSE PEOPLE IN WASHINGTON

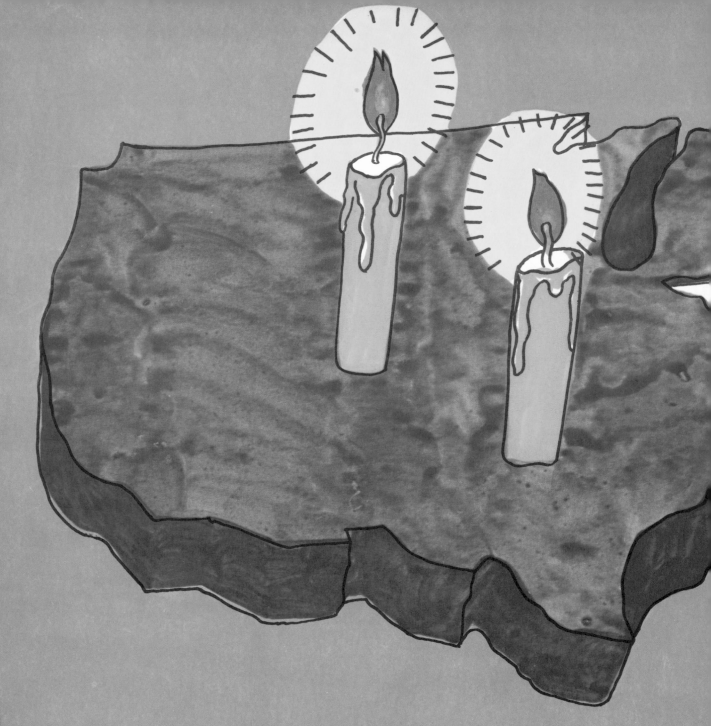

The United States of America is part of the North American continent. It became a nation in 1776. It will be two hundred years old in 1976.

For many years the people of the world came to North America looking for land to settle, or colonize.

The groups coming from England started colonies along the northeastern coast of North America.

These English, or British, colonies were ruled by King George of England. He sent governors to represent him.

England and the king were so far away that some colonists decided it would be better to govern themselves.

In 1776 a group of people from the British colonies wrote the Declaration of Independence. In this they gave the king their reasons for wishing to be independent, or free to form their own government and make their own rules.

The king and the British people did not want to lose their colonies by giving them their independence.

To win their independence, the colonists had to fight a war with the British. It was called the Revolutionary War. The colonists won the war. They were free to form their own government.

They chose the name "state" for the land areas where they lived, worked, played, and learned.

They decided to call their new country, made up of all thirteen states, the United States of America.

As enough people moved into new areas of land, they joined together and formed other states and became part of the United States.

Some of the states are large. Some of the states are small. Some states have many people and some states have only a few. Today there are fifty states.

During the Revolutionary War the colonists had written some rules for governing themselves. They called them the Articles of Confederation. Soon after the war, the people found that these rules were not strong enough to form a good government.

In the year 1787 a group of the people met in Philadelphia to form a stronger government. They wrote a new set of rules. In these new rules each state agreed to give more power to a central government. These rules are called the Constitution. The government they form is called the federal government.

When the new states chose the federal government for the whole country they believed that all the states together were more important than any one state was by itself.

The people who wrote the Constitution knew that in the future rules would have to be changed or added.

The first ten changes were made to be sure that the rights of all the people in all the states would be protected.

These first ten changes, or amendments, were called the Bill of Rights.

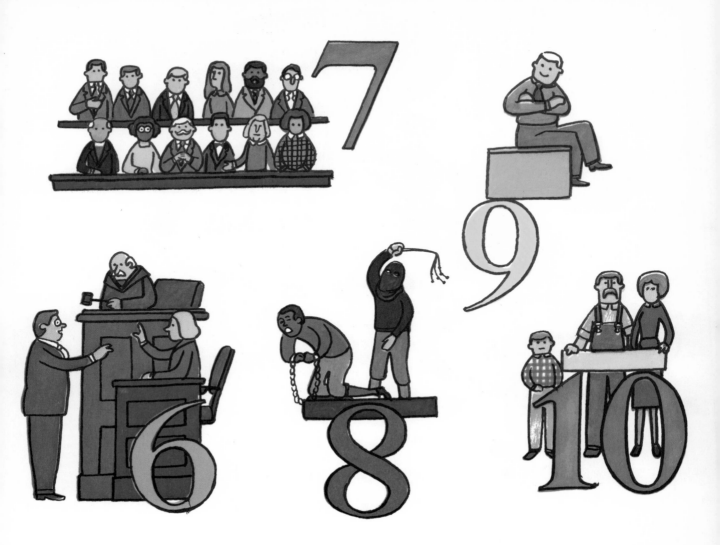

The Constitution said that the federal government would be chosen by the people of the United States. When the people agreed to obey the Constitution they also agreed to choose a government.

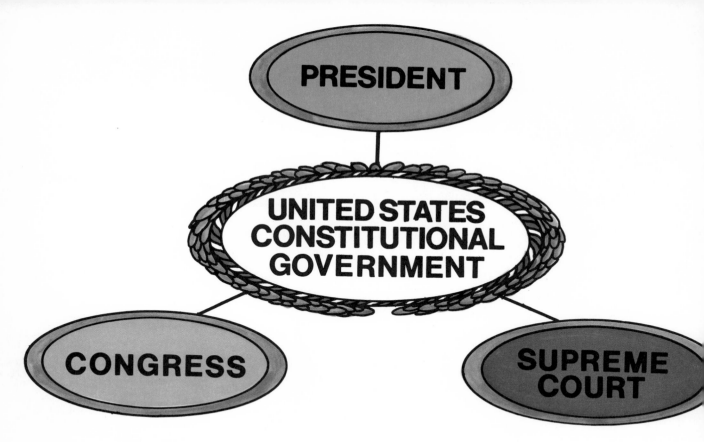

The government formed by the Constitution has three parts, or branches:

- Congress (the legislative branch),
- the President (the executive branch),
- the Supreme Court (the judicial branch).

The people in the federal government work in Washington, D.C.

The Constitution organized Congress first.

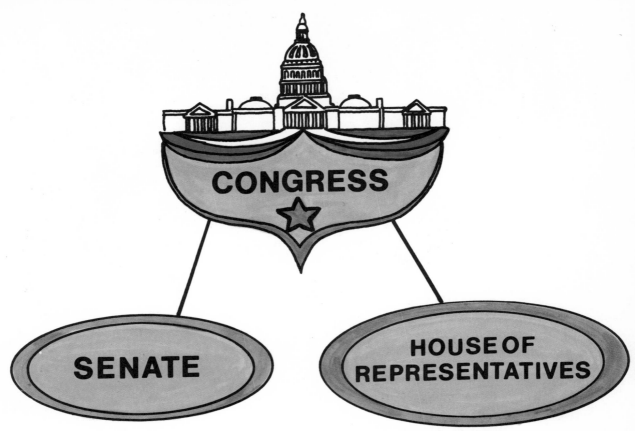

Congress is the legislative branch of the federal government. It has two parts.

One is the Senate.

The other is the House of Representatives.

The home of the Congress is the Capitol Building.

Each state sends people to Congress. These people speak for all the people of their state.

Each state sends two people to the Senate. They are called senators.

All fifty states have different populations (numbers of people), but in the Senate each state counts the same as every other state. No matter how large or how small is the population of a state, each one has two senators. Each senator serves for six years.

One hundred senators represent the fifty states.

17

THE HOUSE OF
REPRESENTATIVES

The House of Representatives is different from the Senate.

States with large populations vote for and send many people to the House of Representatives.

States with small populations vote for and send fewer people to the House of Representatives.

In the House, the states with many people have more to say about rules for the whole country than do states with few people.

By law, there can never be more than 435 representatives.

Each state is divided into areas, or districts, that represent a certain number of people. In this way the states with large populations are divided into many more districts than states with small populations.

The people of each district choose, or vote for, only one representative. They vote for a person who will stand up for,

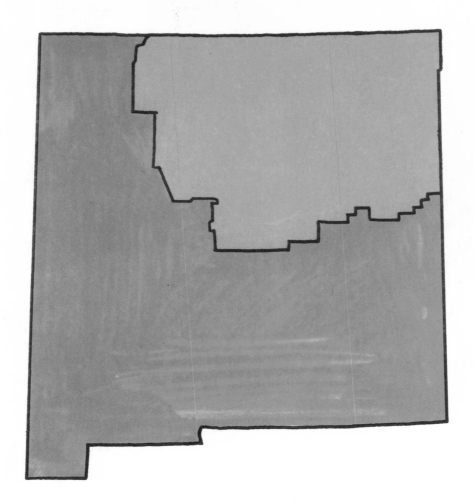

or represent, what they think is best for their district, their state, and the country.

Whoever gets the most votes becomes the representative for his district for two years.

The Congress is responsible for the new rules or laws of the country.

Many people bring ideas to the Congress.

Members of the Senate; members of the House of Representatives; and the president, through his representatives, all bring ideas to the Congress.

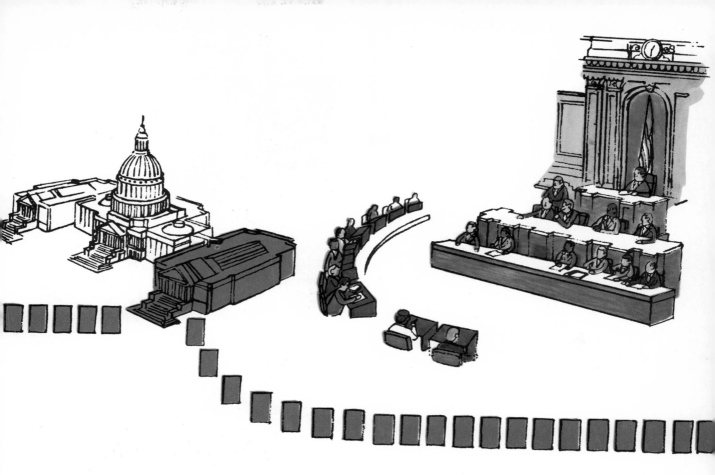

When a new idea, or bill, is presented to the Senate, the senators talk about the bill. They may make some changes in it. Then they vote. If more than one-half of the senators agree to the new bill, we say it has passed the Senate.

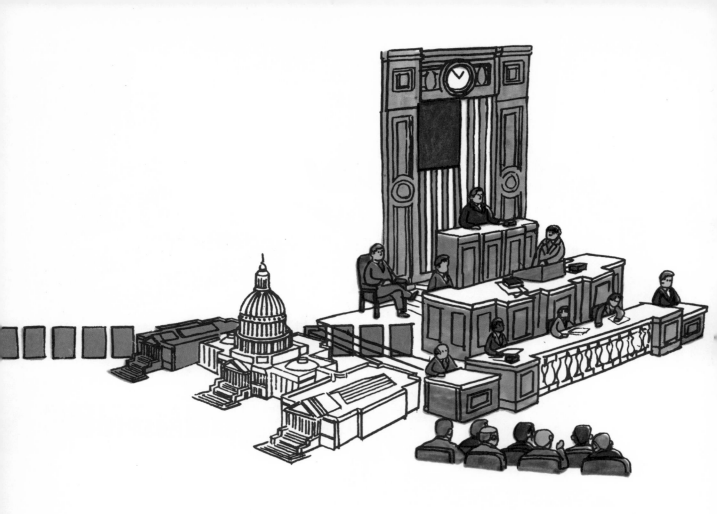

The idea is then presented to the House of Representatives as a new bill.

The representatives talk about the new bill. Then they vote. If more than one-half agree, the bill has passed the House.

After both the Senate and the House
have passed the new bill, the senators
and representatives discuss any dif-
ferences they may still have. If they can
agree on a final bill, they send the bill to
the president.

The president is responsible for the executive branch of the government.

If he agrees to the new bill, he signs it and it becomes a law.

It is his job to make sure that the new law and all the other laws of the country are obeyed.

The president, who lives in the White House, does many things.

He offers ideas to Congress to make the United States a better place in which to live. He tries to convince Congress and the people that the ideas he presents should be tried.

He meets the leaders of other countries, or nations. He is in charge of the army, the navy, the air force, and the marine corps.

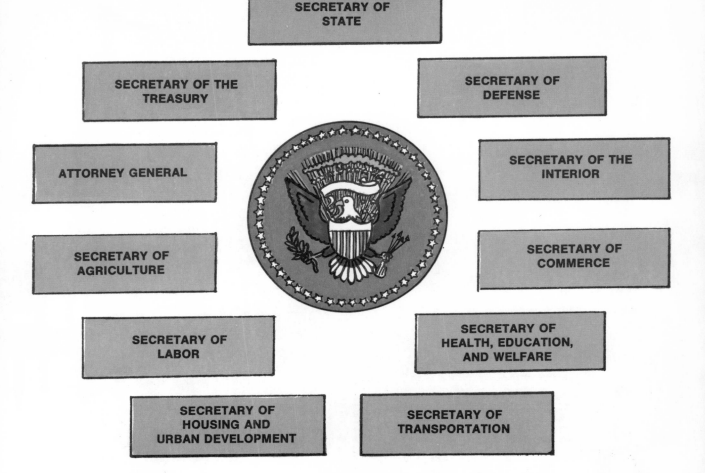

The president has a group of helpers, or advisers, called the Cabinet.

Most members of the Cabinet are called secretaries or ministers.

Each adviser helps the president develop new ideas and carry out his many duties.

The third branch of the government of
the United States is called the Supreme
Court. It is the judicial branch.

There are nine judges, or justices, on the Supreme Court. One is the chief justice and the other eight are associate justices.

When a justice is chosen, he may serve the court for the rest of his life. If a justice retires or dies, the president chooses a new one with the help of the Senate.

All the people are protected by the Constitution from unfair laws. If a person thinks that a law is unfair to him, he may go to the Supreme Court.

The person tells the Supreme Court why he thinks the law is unfair. Then the government tells the Supreme Court why it thinks the law *is* fair.

It is the Supreme Court's job to decide whether the law is fair or unfair.

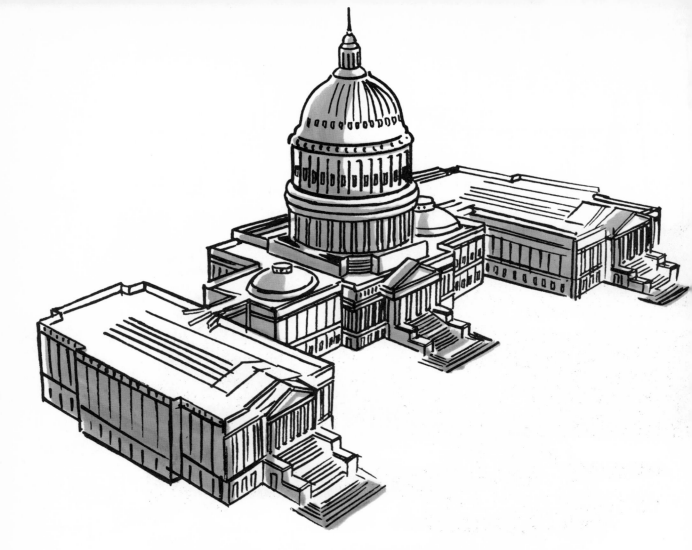

These, then, are the three parts, or branches, of the federal government of the United States:

● The Congress, or legislative branch of the government, with a Senate and a House of Representatives;

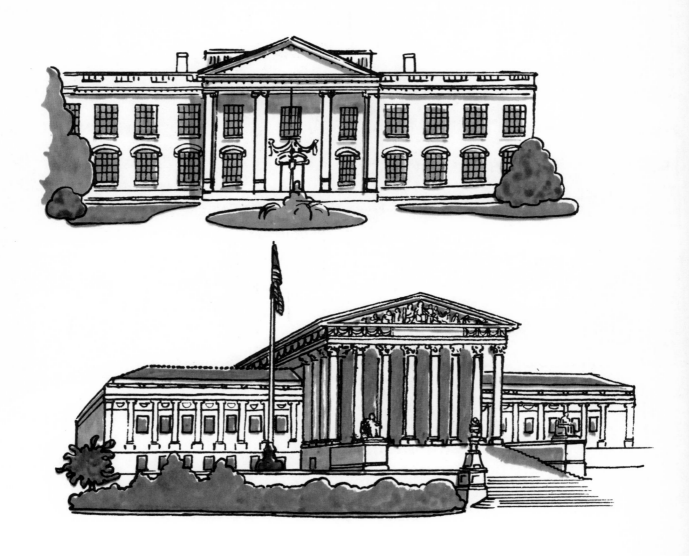

- the President, or executive branch;
- the Supreme Court, or judicial branch.

Now we should discuss how the people choose the members of the federal government.

On the same day in November every four years the people of the country who are eighteen years old or older and who have registered to vote may vote for the president and other members of the government.

We call this an election.

PRESIDENT

VICE PRESIDENT

SENATOR

REPRESENTATIVE

24,569003
24,569004
24,569005
24,569006
24,569007
24,569008
24,569009
24,569010

People who want to be elected part of the federal government put their names on a list called a ballot.

We call the people listed on the ballot candidates. We say they are "running for office."

The ballot may be a piece of paper with blank boxes next to each name, or it may be a voting machine ballot with a lever next to each name.

Usually, two or more people run for each office in the federal government.

The voter picks the one person he thinks will do the best job for each office.

On a paper ballot he marks an X with a pencil or a pen. On a voting machine ballot the X is made by pulling a lever.

For each job, the person with the most votes wins.

The people who are listed on the ballot usually have been chosen by political parties.

A political party is a large group of people with many of the same ideas about the best ways to run the government.

The two largest political parties in the United States are the Democratic Party and the Republican Party.

Most voters belong to one of these two parties.

Other smaller political parties also choose candidates to run for president and other political offices.

41

Some time before the election the political parties have meetings called conventions. Many party members, called delegates, attend the convention. They choose, or nominate, someone to be their representative, or candidate, for president of the country.

At the same convention they also choose their candidate for vice-president. If the president dies, the vice-president becomes the president.

On election day, the people of the
country vote for one of the candidates for
president. The voters will choose the
man who will be president for the next
four years.

If you want to know more about the government of the United States, write to your senator or representative. He or she will be glad to answer your questions.

Keep asking questions and remember that the government of the United States belongs to all the people. It belongs to you.

About the Author: A political science graduate from the University of Maine, David P. Flitner has been writing for several years. *Those People in Washington*, his first childrens book, grew out of his attempts to explain his work in the 1972 presidential primaries to his younger sister. But his life does not revolve only around politics—he is also involved with music. He has performed with various rock groups and now writes and records his own songs.

About the Artist: William Neebe believes that we can create a more humanistic future for our children by providing them with the most comprehensive education possible. One way he tries to accomplish this goal is through his illustrations. He hopes to increase the reader's comprehension through this visual communications technique. A designer and producer of films and other educational matter, he has also served on the Illinois District 37 school board and is currently a member of the New Trier High School Board of Education.